LISTEN UP

Life Lessons from Strangers

Emilie Spaulding

Copyright 2023 by Emilie Spaulding
All Rights Reserved.

CONTENTS

Maya Angelou, poet and activist, describes her pathway from a difficult childhood to becoming a beloved writer. She personally shares her life lesson on how to gain the attention of any restive audience by waiting, winning people's attention, and in her case, wowing them with her poetry and charm. **Page 1**

Sam Reid, fund-raiser extraordinaire, reminds me of the story of the pied piper who gets people to follow him. In Sam's case, people are enthralled to support his cause, saving an historic Wood Island Life Saving Station at the entrance to the Portsmouth, N.H. harbor. One of his life lessons is to make the work fun following the example of Tom Sawyer. Sam has found strangers who will beg to help, insist on happily participating, and entice their friends to do so as well. **Page 11**

Sharon Jones, renowned singer, relates the hurt of prejudice from being the only Black person in her kindergarten class in Portsmouth, NH in the 1950s. Then comes her joy of singing to audiences all over the world. Her life lessons from her own experiences apply to any performer, anywhere, anytime. **Page 19**

Billy Ming Sing Lee, architect, comes from China as a young boy to a NH camp to learn English. He became a Yale architect designing world-renowned buildings. When recently out of architecture school, he designed us a lake house oozing with feng shui on Lake Winnipesaukee, NH. After Billy retired, he successfully promotes friendship between the United States and China, garnering acclaim from both countries. One of his life lessons is that nothing is impossible to do, if you believe you can accomplish the task. **Page 29**

Cameron Kistler, Air Force pilot, applies to the Air Force Academy out of high school, but doesn't get in. He enlists in the Army and fights overseas in dangerous combat for 400 long days. His wife, who was also a pilot, takes care of their three very young children. When he returns, he gets into the Air Force Preparatory School and finally graduates from the Air Force Academy. His life lessons is to never give up on your dreams. **Page 37**

Edwin Caldwell, car salesman, sells you a car, but that is not the end of his friendship. He becomes your friend who will help you in other difficult and/or promising situations. You will be impressed with his ancestors going back four generations. And you can always count on Edwin whenever you need him. **Page 41**

Bill Jeffries, peace advocate and minister, gave advice to people who were repulsed by war. He helped them commit their lives to public service and peace efforts instead. One day the federal agent whose job had been to tap Bill's peace-related telephone for our government, for two years, told Bill he had quit his job and joined the peace effort as a result of listening to Bill's phone calls. **Joanne Jeffries**, Bill's wife, engineered passage of a federal law providing financial aid for the first time to families who have an autistic child and who qualify. **Page 51**

Ken, dump and recycling manager, tells his story of how he befriends customers by being proactive in solving their problems and calling his 2,300 weekly customers by their first names. Ken makes everything seem fun as he shares his pride in a job well done by him and his staff members. **Page 59**

Tom and Joe, anonymous Memorial Bridge workers, in Portsmouth, NH, saved the life of a man who fell or jumped off Memorial bridge into roiling tides. They persevere, putting their own lives at risk, while tracking and helping the stranger be pulled to safety. Their life lesson is to try to never, ever give up on saving a stranger's life. **Page 63**

Peggy, a wildly successful mediator, meets all opposing parties together. Never, ever, alone. She also meets with both sides in a marriage only concurrently After sharing with us how she manages that difficult feat, she then gives us readers free advice on how to never need counseling, mediating, or legal advice in the first place. This free advice should prevent us readers on both sides, from getting into trouble altogether. **Page 71**

Jean Royer, computer genius and blueberry farmer, thrives at the beginning of the computer era. Upon retirement he plants a startup blueberry business. Customers stop by and pick berries on their own and pay on the honor system. His life lessons are if you care, trust, and treat customers with respect and friendship, they will reciprocate in equal measure. **Page 79**

INTRODUCTION

Wouldn't the world be a better place if we all had more empathy? A caring that comes when we open our arms and hearts and ears.

I've gained wisdom listening to a diverse group of people while writing this memoir, *Listen Up... Life Lessons from Strangers*.

One idea struck me like a thunder bolt! It's important for all of us — whatever our relationship, nationality, or point of view — to talk and listen to each other. We could express our concerns, joys and sorrows, and especially things we would like to change.

Please read on and learn more about these fascinating people.

I hope their suggestions take root and make your life even better.

—Emilie Spaulding, Author

Maya Angelou

Maya's Angelou's Life Lesson:

"Before you enter a room,
  stand tall, hold your head up, walk slowly.
  Wait for everyone to stop talking…
no matter how long it takes!"

Maya Angelou

Our teenaged girls begged me one hot summer day, "Why can't we join the country club that our friends belong to? They go swimming, play tennis and golf, and there are dances."

"I don't think we should!" I answered. Actually, I was paranoid. Would our three girls become snooty, superior, and start treating people of lesser circumstances in a shabby way? I worried about all that.

Plus, when they were little, we had purposely moved to the Tarrytowns, NY, from Brooklyn Heights – since there were children from forty different countries in the new school system. The superintendent had said, "That's in part because we have a General Motors plant here. Our system is called the Princeton plan. And students will move to schools in different neighborhoods every three or four years, so they get to know all sorts of different nationalities." Soon enough, the girls forgot about their country club request and had moved on to something else.

Everything was fine until I read in the Tarrytown Daily News that Maya Angelou would be the guest speaker at a Sleepy Hollow Country Club benefit on Saturday. I so admired her poetry that ebbed and flowed, her chutzpah in trying anything she wanted, and her willingness to take risks no matter what!

The Country Club event would take place on a hill overlooking the Hudson River next to the Rockefeller estate. It

Maya Angelou

was only a mile upriver from our house. I pretended to Dick that the beneficiary of the fund-raiser was the reason for our decision to attend. But for the life of me, now, I don't even remember what that good cause was.

Truthfully, I was happy to pay any price to see and hear Ms. Angelou, even from afar in a crowded ballroom. Dick's main motivation to come was probably to humor me and keep peace at home.

On the night of the event, when it was time for Maya to arrive at the club, I told Dick I was going to the rest room. He didn't know the real reason that I was leaving the table was to try to talk with Ms. Angelou and ask her some questions. I paced back and forth near the entrance hallway. But Maya was half an hour late. I stood alone since the official greeters had temporarily given up and returned to the party to glad-hand wealthy donors.

Suddenly, the outside door opened. Maya walked in. I could see her driver waiting in the car out front. At the ballroom entry where I stood, she paused, took a deep breath, and started walking quickly toward the podium looking right and left. The Emcee and officials rushed up to her saying, "At last. Welcome Ms. Angelou. Thank you so much for coming and helping this good cause. Please follow us."

There would be no possible chance for me to talk to her. "Oh well," I thought.

A hushing sound started echoing around the room. Some people were quieting down. However, out of sight, others kept laughing loudly in two separate wings off the ballroom. These neighbors had been drinking a bit and were getting caught up on the latest news. They paid no mind to the "hushes."

Maya climbed the steps to the podium, smiled and stood there looking at still-chatting guests. She didn't say a word. She didn't look annoyed. What seemed like five minutes ticked by.

Embarrassed people who were paying attention – shushed louder. One person, with a high-pitched voice I'd recognize to this day, kept chatting and gesturing. They were at last getting caught up with friends and neighbors they hadn't seen for a while. Probably, by now, they had finished a discussion of where their kids were going to college, and which had graduated or gotten married. Ms. Angelou shifted her feet, standing still on the podium while people looked at their watches. Maya still smiled and not once did she glance at her timepiece.

When silence finally held sway, Ms. Angelou talked about the importance of the cause. And her appreciation for our support. The crowd clapped loud, long, and lovingly. The emcee gushed a hearty, "Thank you!"

Maya headed back toward the outside door and her driver, walking slowly and nodding to the crowd on each side. They parted as if she were a queen. But no one was brave enough to stop this force of nature and say anything. Not one person out of almost a hundred guests.

Maya Angelou

Shy me, knowing this would be my only chance ever to talk with her, followed behind until we were approaching the exit. I really did want to meet her. Being the cautious person I was then, I was startled to hear my voice say, "Ms. Angelou, may I ask you a personal question?"

"Of course." She stopped walking and looked me straight in the eye.

"Would you tell me how to command attention in a crowded, noisy room the way you just did? And would you mind sharing your secret of getting everyone to treat you with such respect? Do you think even I could bring it off?"

She looked at me as if I were the only person in the room, actually, the only person in the world who mattered, and asked, "What's your name?"

I told her, "Emilie."

"Emilie, it's easy. Just stop and collect yourself at the doorway before you go in. Stand tall. Hold your head up. Walk slowly. Most importantly, once there, wait for *everyone* to stop talking. No matter how long it takes. Never start until it's completely silent. And yes, you can do it! *Believe that you can. I'm confident that you will!*"

"Thank you so much for your advice!" I said. "I'll do it!"

I decided I'd take to heart what she had said. After all, I had promised.

Maya nodded to smitten me. "Bye, now," she smiled and was still walking regally as she went out the door to her waiting driver.

Emilie Spaulding

Her advice reminded me of long-ago advice from my mother in Alabama. "Toots," she had said, "When you walk into a room don't rush in flustered. Stop, wait, hold your head up and pretend you have a sparkling jewel on your chest that you want everyone to see. Then stroll. You do know how to stroll, don't you?"

"Yes Ma'am," I had said, although I didn't really know how to stroll at all. My having three daughters in four and a half years, girls that I had to keep track of day and night, hadn't left me any time to practice strolling. But after hearing Maya's advice, I would definitely saunter when arriving at an event, where someone I could learn something from might be speaking. Why I would even practice in the grocery store, walking down the street, and at home.

After that auspicious night, I've followed the counsel of Maya and Mother, whose lives were so different from each other. Their advice works if one has the patience and courage to remember to wait until a room is as quiet as a church on a Monday morning.

After that event, I've started to talk to any stranger who looked as if they had an important lesson that I could write down and share with you.

And, each time I accost a stranger, it becomes easier to do it again and again. The responses and life lessons of ten other interesting strangers can be found in the rest of this book.

After Maya left, in a flush of gratitude at that same event

Maya Angelou

I bought for our oldest daughter, Amy, a signed poem by Ms. Angelou. It now hangs on her wall in North Carolina. It sums up Maya's spirit and reads...

Phenomenal Woman

I say, It's in the reach of my arms,
The span of my hips,
The stride of my step,
The curl of my lips.
 I'm a woman
 Phenomenally.
 Phenomenal woman,
 That's me.
I say
It's the fire in my eyes,
And the flash of my teeth,
The swing in my waist,
And the joy in my feet.
I'm a woman
Phenomenally.
Phenomenal woman,
That's me.

Maya's poem fit her perfectly. Maybe it also fits me and the other women in our family. Might they laugh and try it too? Or would they simply say, "Our crazy relative!"

Now that Maya is gone, I want to pass along her life lessons to you.

Now I know, anyone can get an audience to become quiet and hear your advice. I think she knew I would take her advice. And she would be pleased to know that you might follow her advice too.

"May you rest in peace, Maya."

Note: In 1991, 10 years later, phenomenal tennis player Arthur Ashe would be the first Black person to join that very same Sleepy Hollow Country Club. Two of our daughters had left for college and our girls' new friends continued to come from all over the world. "Mom," they say, "do you know the best thing you ever did for us?"

"Cook and wash 8,242 dishes every year?" I replied.

"No, it was to insist that we grow up and get to know people from all over the world and learn to care about them and their differences."

Maya Angelou

In 1993, Ms. Angelou became the first African American woman in U.S. history to recite the presidential inaugural poem for a President, Bill Clinton, at his swearing in.

And in 2022, Maya became the first African American woman to appear on a U.S. quarter.

Sam Reid

"Remember Tom Sawyer and make work look like fun. People will plead to help you."

—Sam Reid, Preservationist and Extraordinary Fund Raiser

Sam Reid

Sam Reid, from the Maine/New Hampshire seacoast, although middle-aged, looks like a teenager frozen in time. With his straight dark hair under a worn white cap, matching slacks, a weary-looking life jacket, and plastic Crocs that expel water through tiny holes, you might be fooled. All of this is topped by a genial grin.

But it wasn't always this way, Sam reports. "A big difficulty when I was younger was that I was very short and small. It was no fun in grade school and boarding in high school since other students called me names. I felt insecure. Then, thankfully I found rowing and became the coxswain. Being lightweight as a coxswain was a huge benefit. My years as a boy in Maine dealing with boats was excellent, since I became the captain of the crew. All of this meant I spent a lot of time on the water, which fueled my love for everything related to watercraft.

"After college, at 20 I worked for Bear Stearns on the floor of the New York Stock Exchange. I gave up coffee since one didn't need an additional stimulant. There were no chairs since we didn't have the time or space to sit down. The life lesson from that job, which has stayed with me, is being able to perform under pressure. And take orders accurately. No mistakes were allowed. I learned people can be kind under their stern facade. And if an employee met all the requirements, our sense of extended family was powerful.

Sam Reid

"Through the years I have been fortunate to speak at college graduations since I love public speaking. The message I try to communicate is to encourage new graduates to do public service and help others. I must have been listening as well as talking back then, since I follow my own advice."

You might notice Sam's warm smile camouflages his persistence and drive to save historic sites. He is determined to accomplish seemingly impossible goals. His persuasion in convincing strangers of any shape, size, or sympathy to care and donate to his preservation causes is awesome. People who know him well say Sam is a force of nature, like the Atlantic Ocean waves that crash against shoreline, boulders, and boats on Maine's coast.

Navigation between the New Hampshire/Maine seacoasts was perilous in olden days when primitive lighthouses and flags, flares, and flimsy charts were the only safety measures. Seafarers from afar, as well as local fishermen, sometimes lost their boats, or even worse, their lives.

Help came in 1908. A lifesaving station plus sea walls and a marine railway to launch rowing rescue boats were built on Wood Island. In howling gales, the island station Sam and others are now hellbent on saving was a beacon of hope for sailors in trouble, plying roiling waves. Survivors who made it were thankful for the fortitude and bravery of surfmen working and stationed on Wood Island. Being part of the U.S. Life Saving service was not for the faint of heart.

Often, Wood Islanders would risk their own lives making rescues in eight-oared surfboats.

During WWII, Wood Island workers played additional roles – as lookouts for Nazi U-boats hoping to attack Portsmouth Naval Station upriver. A seaman's job included opening and closing a massive underwater chain-link fence. It was an unbelievable half mile in length, and over 80 feet tall. It stretched across the river between Maine and New Hampshire. Besides keeping people out, the fence also allowed local traffic to navigate the waters when it was opened for them.

Sam reports, "The advent of modern equipment such as ship-to-shore radios, radar, and GPS changed things. Wood Island was decommissioned in 1948 and the U.S. Coast Guard moved into a new facility in New Castle, New Hampshire, on dry land, which was easier to access.

The island's building, sea walls, dock, and surroundings began to decline, decay, and deteriorate into an eyesore. Government officials in Kittery, Maine were determined to remove everything from the island, returning the land to its natural environment, which would require minimal upkeep."

A bugle must have sounded. Sam began leading a vanguard of people wanting to save, restore, and remember the Wood Island Life Saving Station. Some people involved were descendants of nearby families, such as Sam's ancestors who have lived in the area for centuries.

Sam Reid

They joined locals and political officials, historical preservationists, and environmentalists. All were convinced it was a futuristically important idea to set up a nonprofit Wood Island Life Saving Station Association, (WILSSA). Their goal was to raise millions of dollars to restore the island and station to its historic lifesaving glory. The island would then become a place for school children and others to visit and learn about past rescues and to celebrate the dedication to duty of the brave men of the sea.

To get approvals, Sam contacted government officials on every level. Sam arranged for WILSSA to become a qualified 501(c)(3) recipient for receiving gifts.

An incredible highlight has been the partnership with the Maine Army National Guard. With the help of former U.S. Coast Guard Commandant Jim Loy and former U.S. Secretary of Defense, William Cohen, WILSSA was able to convince Maine's Major General Douglas Farnham to order his troops to come to Wood Island for their annual training. The Guard built sea walls on the island. Ho hum you might think. But the chore took two platoons of 60 men and women, working seven days a week for a month in 2018, in 2019, and a partial month in 2020.

Try to imagine, if you can, the logistical challenge of getting 45 huge concrete trucks to the tiny island to pour the sea wall's base. There are other brave and inspiring stories. And everyone's effort is appreciated.

I asked Sam what additional *life lessons* he has learned

and asked him to give tips for readers to use in our own challenging endeavors.

Sam stated, **"Life Lesson One:** is *The Tom Sawyer Effect*. Remember the story when Tom Sawyer had a huge fence to whitewash, a punishment from his Aunt Polly for skipping school? She wanted to teach Tom a lesson. Tom despaired, wondering how in the world he could accomplish painting such a long fence alone." Sam continued, "I've learned and did what Tom did. He called on acquaintances, encouraged participation of friends, and made any work incredibly fun when people did participate."

Life Lesson Two: "Tom convinced his friends that painting the fence was a *privilege, not a chore*. Tom's friends went from skeptical to eager to begging to participate. They even gave Tom gifts to convince him to let them help," Sam explained. In exactly that same vein, Sam's friends visited the island, attended fundraisers, and donated gifts of money to WILSSA. Sam's friends happened to include elected and governmental officials on the federal, regional, state, and local levels. These friends helped him garner necessary approvals, find funding sources, and locate grants to donate to the cause. Sam says his mantra was, *"It will be a privilege and make you feel happy when you donate to WILSSA."*

Sam Reid

Life Lesson Three: Sam also makes people feel as if they are part of a historical continuum. Island visitors often mention what a good time they had on trips to Wood Island in a small historic boat.

They look ahead to being able to schedule overnight stays, personal events, and weddings on Wood Island. They will then have photographs of important events in their own lives on historic Wood Island.

Another local reported, "On every visit, WILSSA guests are soothed with conversation, cocktails, and congeniality. Back home, other donors meet at friends' houses for get-together parties, discussions, and to hear an inspiring pep talk."

Sam concludes, "Together we are not only preserving the important history of Wood Island rescues for school children and adults from far away. We are also creating and recording our own historic events as well." The WILSSA saga continues.

Emilie Spaulding

Wood Island Life Saving Station Renovation

Sharon Jones

"Always say I'm sorry, say I love you, and calling on the phone does not count."

—Sharon Jones, Singer Extraordinaire

Sharon Jones

Petite Sharon Jones in a sleek black dress smiled at our New Hampshire church congregation. When she began to sing, her surprisingly strong voice rattled the rafters; pounded ancient pews; and rushed past wavy-glass windows. And if her voice didn't warm us up on this blustery Sunday, the clapping hands of dyed-in-the-wool northerners did.

Some among us, thought, "I don't want this to end." We sent up prayers, "Dear God, please stop time so I can clap to music rather than go home and cook Sunday dinner." Sharon awakened the meek and the bold, the young and the old, and everyone in between.

Sharon had followed her childhood dream to sing. Since I thought she would be an interesting stranger to write about, I called her a week or so after her performance, "Hi Sharon, it's Emilie. May I write a chapter about you in my book which might be called, *Twelve Life Lessons You'll Love*."

I held my breath, crossed my fingers, and bit my tongue. "Why not?" she said.

But then she undid my new loyalty…"Emilie, I remember you, you're that *camp follower* who helped me carry my microphone out to the car after the church service."

I was incensed to be called a camp follower. To my mind that was derogatory. To me, that word meant an overbearing fan. So, I thought of hanging up.

Sharon Jones

But you must know that I will swallow my pride and put up with anything to get a story I want, anywhere, anytime.

When I saw her again, I mentioned in passing, that I considered someone calling me a camp follower – meant I was a pest.

Sharon said, "Oh, sorry! That means an interested fan to me."

So we moved beyond that. I asked her where her musical talent came from.

"My mother Ethel played classical music and my father Harry played jazz, and anything by Louis Armstrong. Daddy entertained troops during World War II, in the early 1940s, as did Bob Hope. But I learned the most from listening to musicians who came to our house, every Sunday afternoon to jam. As a young girl of four or five, I'd sit on the steps and listen, and learn, and tap my foot.

"But I became a singer by accident. Sister Lucy sang on the radio every weekend in Portsmouth. When Lucy was introduced on the air, I knew it would be safe to sneak into her room, put on her dress clothes, and heels, and sing along. I pretended I was on the air. When Lucy stopped singing at the station, I'd rush back, and stuff her clothes and shoes back where I'd found them. Lucy was my role model."

I asked Sharon, had there been any bad times?

"Yes! I was the only Black person in my kindergarten class at New Franklin Elementary in Portsmouth in 1949.

Emilie Spaulding

That was five years before the US Supreme Court's Brown v. Board of Education ruling ended racial segregation in public schools.

"Every morning my mother, our dog Rex, and I would walk to school. I felt awful that no one would hold my hand when we made a circle at school. No one would ever stand next to me when we lined up. No one would play with me at recess. No one wanted to be around me, ever. Was it all because I had dark skin?

"I was so upset, at six, I decided to take this hurtful treatment into my own hands. I started slipping out of school and Rex and I would walk home and say, 'Surprise!' to my mother. Soon, mother went to talk to the teacher. I sat and waited and waited at a tiny desk in the hallway. Strangely, they came out smiling and nodding. Mother wouldn't tell me why.

"Next day there was a huge box on my desk. Now I had something no one else did. Inside was a doll with a wooden face, who I called Tootie. Tootie became my buddy in class. At lunch. On the playground.

"Finally, I had a friend! Rex and I didn't have to make any more unscheduled trips home."

I asked Sharon, "Did anyone else ever help you deal with tough school situations?

"Yes!" she said, "Nine years later, at fifteen. I joined the chorus at newly built Portsmouth High School. Music Director, Mr. Elwell, was amazed at my powerful voice. He asked me to sing the final song at each year's Portsmouth H.S. Clipper Minstrel Show.

"We had a 30-piece orchestra and a choir, which attracted people from all over the seacoast to our performances. "The audience went crazy with applause when I sang the closing song after my freshman, sophomore, and junior years.

"But it did upset me that the choir sang with black faces painted on with shoe polish. And we had big red clown-like mouths painted on with lipstick. To Black people, someone doing black face is making fun of our race.

"Then…at the end of my senior year of high school, after they announced I would be singing the closing song, the heavy curtains opened. Try as I may I could not make myself go out on the stage. My feet wouldn't move."

"'What's wrong?' Mr. Elwell asked calmly.

"'It's the black faces of the choir.'

"He called for an intermission. He closed the curtains.

"When the curtains opened again, and I came onstage, the choir's clean-scrubbed faces shone.

"I still remember I sang, *Just the way you look.*

"When they closed the curtains, I had tears in my eyes. Mr. Elwell did too. The audience stood and applauded me. Was it because it was my last time to sing? Or was it because I had stood my ground? Regardless, the applause sounded like a squadron of fighter airplanes buzzing overhead. I felt so happy.

Emilie Spaulding

"The musical program, from then on was called, Portsmouth H.S. Clipper Show. Mr. Elwell gave me a cassette of the last performance I had sung. I still have it to this day. The time frame was four years after Martin Luther King, Jr. met with civil rights leaders in Atlanta to coordinate nonviolent protests against racial discrimination."

I asked Sharon where she got her initiative to try new things. She explained, "From watching my father work two jobs – as an electrician during the day, as a musician at night and on weekends.

"When he went to someone's house to fix an electrical problem, if customers did not speak English he could speak enough of their language for them to understand. He had learned French, Spanish, German, and bits of other languages in the army. He somehow found a solution to any problem. So I've tried to copy him.

"Next, I wanted to start singing with the renowned Johnny Hammond group who played jazz on the organ. His album, *Breakout*, had been released in 1971. Before my father gave his approval, he told Johnny, 'Sharon can go. But if you touch one hair on her head, I'll....' Johnny lived up to that unspoken agreement and I toured for two years, all over the United States."

I asked Sharon if she would share some performance tips with us.

She didn't hesitate, "When the MC announces your name, sing or play immediately, a snappy show-stopper tune. After you grab the crowd's attention, they will be with you for the rest of the night. But don't stop feeding them what they love. I think this would work for any kind of performance."

Next, I asked Sharon how she decides which songs to sing in bars vs churches vs concerts.

"I've learned to keep a menu of songs for each venue. To come up with the right songs I keep track of what people at the different places react to, clap the loudest for, or request the next time. Pretty soon, It's easy.

"I pull out separate music menus that are tested, tried and true. Other performers might try that."

I wanted to know, "Did you ever take formal lessons or were you self-taught?"

"I moved to Los Angeles to study music so I could perform professionally. At that time, it was difficult for me to reach all octaves. A friend connected me with a vocal coach at the Gilbert and Sullivan Conservatory, whose name was Rusty. She said, 'Sharon if you are serious about music, I'll work with you. But if you are going to hang out, smoke, and drink, don't waste my time. Which is it?'"

Sharon said, "All I could think of was, Good Lord, where's the sweet old lady I thought would meet me at the door saying, 'Come on in?' Lessons were tough, but I learned to sing with less effort, to use breath control, and know how to store air. It made me want to go farther on my musical journey. I would recommend other musicians try lessons to make performing easier.

"Still, I yearned to be the main singer out front. So I came home and was the main attraction with my brother's band, working the Catskills in summers, and Montreal and Boston the rest of the year."

I asked Sharon, "What keeps you singing and performing until the wee hours, night after night, week after week? Did you ever start to think of retiring?"

"There is an incredibly wonderful feeling after you put your heart and soul and technique into singing your favorite songs. When you finish, a crowd of people jump up and clap and yell encouragement, and whistle and stomp. They usually ask you to play another song.

"It is hard to describe what that is like for a musician. So, as long as that happens, I will be there, singing my heart out, night after night."

Sharon constantly mentioned how her family had encouraged each other. To me, their life advice holds equal weight with her musical memories and counsel.

Sharon explained, "My family has a unique set of rules:"

Life Lesson One: "Always say I'm sorry if you hurt anyone's feelings. Always, and as soon as possible."

Life Lesson Two: "Say I love you, lots of times, but especially before going to bed."

Sharon Jones

Life Lesson Three: "Go and visit if someone is having a difficult time and bring flowers. Calling on the phone does not count."

I applaud Sharon and her family for bringing music, joy, and friendship to family, friends, and strangers and for her being an example of someone who knew what career she wanted and stuck with it.

Most of all, I urge others to gently tell people when they annoy you. I'm so glad I did. Sharon and I got over that camp follower comment and have become close friends.

Billy Ming Sing Lee

"Nothing is Impossible. Just do it!"

—Billy Ming Sing Lee, architect

Billy Ming Sing Lee

Summer weekends and vacations my husband Dick would leave his executive veep job at Scholastic Inc. in NYC where his brother was President. I would leave my job as administrative assistant at Raymond Loewy/William Snaith, an industrial design firm – but, alas, none of my relatives worked there. Since Dick and I had been married, we'd head straight to the Spaulding compound on Lake Winnipesaukee, NH on summer weekends.

In 1967, the Spaulding family matriarch Caroline walked down a winding pine-needled path to a cabin called Battsford, where Dick and I now stayed with our three-and-a-half-year-old daughter Amy and her sister Susan, two. Kristiana wasn't born yet. Caroline knocked robustly on the cabin door. "It's time for you to build a house somewhere on the property," she said to Dick and me. "The younger generations can then move in here." I looked for a smile of encouragement but... I must have glanced away too soon.

Then came the struggle of what style house to build. Everyone else in Dick's family had built a one-story cabin with three rooms, a kitchen, and a bath. For modesty, a tiny dressing room had been added, popular in the 1930s. An open deck with wooden railing and a hemlock hedge ran across the front, facing the lake.

All the cabins had been built by family, friends, or a local builder. I had dated Barry, an architecture student when I was a senior in high school in Auburn, Alabama. One thing

Billy Ming Sing Lee

I learned from him was: "Always use an architect. Your home will meld into the site, be at one with nature, and have an artistic persona."

Dick finally did agree to use an architect. But he insisted that we hire a recent graduate since he'd be cheaper than an experienced one.

It turned out to be perfect advice when an old friend suggested we use Billy Ming Sing Lee, recently graduated from Yale School of Architecture. Billy asked a perfect question of a sailor like Dick, "Which way does the fair wind come from?"

Billy explained his history, "I came as a young boy from China in 1978 to Camp Wyandotte in Wolfeboro, New Hampshire, to learn to speak English. It wasn't easy.

"One of the boys kicked me in the rear and said, 'Go home Chinaman!' I smiled at him and said, 'I play soccer too. Where do you play?' My not getting upset seemed to disarm any bully.

"Later on, some of my colleagues would say, 'Ming Sing?' I'd ask if he wanted me to sing 'Yankee Do Do Dandy?' They'd laugh. It would be over. My life lesson attitude has always been, instead of reprimanding someone we should be positive and help each other."

Years later, Billy confessed to me just how he decided where on the 30 acres to site our house. He said, "Dick's brother, Johnny, flew us to the lake in his single engine plane. The weather was wicked. The tiny plane was buffeted by erratic, howling winds, and driving rain. Even Johnny's shirt was wet with sweat from exasperation, exertion, and fear."

Billy continued, "Finally, when the plane flew over the Spaulding property, I looked down and immediately fell in love with one huge rock jutting out from the lakeside. I reasoned that the whole purpose of having a property beside a lake is to become part of the environment – storms, tranquility, wind, sunlight, smell, and sound. In my mind, the first location I saw was the only choice.

"But, thinking you might not appreciate such an esoteric reason, I told you it would be best to build at either end of the property. Then the thirty other members of the family wouldn't be trooping by the house constantly."

Decades later, Billy confessed to the true reason for his choice. A gigantic tree leaned over the water, tallest of all the trees on the shore. It was footed with huge boulders jutting into the water. At that moment, while still seated in the buffeting plane, Billy said he had decided to make the house resemble a huge rock, angled, as if in conversation with the tallest tree. And when the time came, the house was built precisely like that.

Billy continued, "Another challenge was locating the windows. Some must look up to the sky and clouds, others out to the lake, and others down at the ground/flowers/and pine needles."

Dick remembers Billy's very first visit – the one with bad

weather – eight people were cramped together in one bedroom and the living room in the Battsford cabin. Later, remembering back to that day, Billy designed our new house with one great room. The stairway in the middle of the room created four different work or play spaces in the corners: the kitchen, the living room, the dining area, and a music space. Billy had solved future "too many people in one room" problems beautifully.

I remember when the house was actually constructed, everything was just as Billy had drawn it on a piece of paper. Every tree and rock was exactly where Billy had sketched them.

At the beginning of the building process, a funny incident happened. John Viano, was an experienced old-style local builder who had won the construction bid. The blueprint and plans that Billy gave John had a section of detailed specifications and instructions, including directions on exactly how to hammer the nails.

Billy, a graduate of Yale Architecture school, who had interned with the famous I. M. Pei, had explained in minute detail how he wanted the house boards to be nailed in. For new builders it might have been important information. And John, an experienced builder, did seem to be paying attention. Then Billy asked, "John, why aren't you writing down any of this important information?"

"I have a good memory, it'll be okay."

Billy insisted, "Please write it down to humor me." So

John wrote everything down with a pencil on a thin piece of construction board. Finally, Billy got into his car and drove away, satisfied things would go well.

As we watched Billy's taillights disappear into the woods, John took his board with his building instructions on it and sailed it into nearby bushes.

As a lone worker, it took John two years to finish the house. John had builder friends come and help him, but only when he had to raise an entire wall. Friends would pick up the top of the wall and hold it, while John would nail it in. Then they all sipped something out of the same bottle, smoked a cigar, and went home waiting for their next call to raise a wall.

Billy from China and John from New England became friends during the two-year building process. They ended up proud of working through their differences and reaching a memorable conclusion – a house that bonds with earth, water, and sky.

As Billy was leaving the almost finished house toward the end, he turned to me and said on a fall day in 1971, "Have you ever heard of feng shui?"

"No," I said, "Why?"

"Someday you'll understand it and how it influenced this house." A few years later, feng shui did become a household word.

Thanks, Billy and John, for working together to create our house oozing feng sui, while bonding with its surroundings, and creating a sense of balance and calm.

Billy, up until his 90s, continued to build important buildings such as museums and public spaces. Since then, Billy has started creating friendships among people in different countries all over the world. The program is aptly named Friendshipology.

Life Lesson One: Be sympathetic to people with different points of view. Instead of reprimanding each other, create a positive environment for helping each other, just as he and John Viano with dissimilar backgrounds accomplished. In the end they were able to work hand in hand. Bravo to them both! And now to Billy for his important work building peace among people of different nationalities.

Emilie Spaulding

Lake house designed by Billy Ming Sing Lee,
built by John Viano.

Cameron Kistler

"Never, ever give up on your mission, passion, or goals!"

—Cameron Kistler, Air Force Pilot

Cameron Kistler

When Cameron Kistler was a young fellow and went to an amusement park, other children enjoyed going on every ride. Cameron, however, stood fascinated watching the gears on the wheels. He always wondered how things with moving parts worked.

He took apart his toys and made new ones. Unlike many people who struggle to decide what they want to be when they grow up, Cameron knew from age 15. He only wanted to be a pilot. This discovery happened when he went to an airshow and was drawn to the power, wonder, and majesty of the Air Force fighter jets. Immediately after graduation from high school, he applied to his dream school, the U.S Air Force Academy. He wasn't accepted, although his sister had been.

Cameron didn't let his disappointment get him down. He followed a quote he learned from his dad, John, "Make short term sacrifices for long term success." That could mean anything, but for Cameron it meant he joined the Army, and deployed with a Military Intelligence Battalion, into a combat zone for 400 days. While there, it was 123 degrees midday, plus whatever heat a helmet, bullet proof vest, and backpack added on. Even in all that heat, his dream of being a pilot never melted.

Once out, he applied again. This time he was accepted to the Air Force Academy Preparatory School. Finally, Cameron was accepted by the Air Force Academy, Class of 2016.

Cameron Kistler

While there, Cameron became part of the Wings of Blue Parachute Team. He jumped out of planes a total of 550 times – at ball games, airshows, and graduations. The students aimed to show off the parachute team's capabilities.

At his graduation from the Academy, Cameron was recognized by President Obama as one of the few graduates who had deployed to combat before coming there to the Academy.

Cameron next took Jet Pilot Training to learn to become an F-16 "Viper" fighter pilot which can take quick turns to outmaneuver enemies. A Viper happens to cost $36 million, can fly at over 1400 miles per hour, and at altitudes of 50,000 feet. It can also carry 510 rounds of 20 mm ammunition to be used in air-to-air combat or air-to-ground engagements. Sometimes it carries air-to-air missiles, as well as air-to-ground munitions including rockets and various types of bombs.

Cameron wore a helmet-mounted cueing system "HMCS" that allows a pilot to keep track of a target in order to run an intercept or engage in basic fighter maneuvers against the adversary. Cameron's location in hot spots around the world was kept a secret.

Cameron planned to continue flying a Viper for as long as possible, due to his enjoyment of flying and his commitment to the United States.

Cameron's wife Sloane and three small children were at home in the states while he flew missions. She says, "I was able to manage the house and kids because Cameron talked me through hard days, made me laugh when things weren't easy, and cheered me on... always."

News Flash: After many years of flying, Cameron and the Air Force have made the decision for him to become an instructor of fighter pilots. He and his wife and children recently moved to an Air Force pilot training school.

Cameron is known at work for saying things like, "Guys, there is no reason to stress, we have the best job in the world!"

Cameron's Life Lesson One: "Make time for your family. Your career will end, but you family lasts forever."

Cameron's Life Lesson Two: "Leave your work at work. When you are at home, be fully at home, mentally and physically."

Cameron's Life Lesson Three: "Find something you enjoy and do it. I believe anyone can accomplish anything if you follow your heart, have courage, and stay motivated. Regardless of your desire to be a fighter pilot, an astronaut, or a Walmart greeter, make your life decisions based on your hopes, aspirations, and goals. And don't let anyone or anything stop you!"

Thanks, Cameron, for inspiring us all to follow our dreams, no matter what might stand in the way.

Edwin Caldwell

"You can become much more than just a salesman – be a friend, helper, and adviser. You will be appreciated, consulted, and rewarded beyond measure."

—*Edwin Caldwell. Supersalesman*

Edwin Caldwell

Do you know people who prefer being with others who have the same background, lifestyle, and attitudes as their own? My sister in Durham, North Carolina might fit that category. However, it was strange, this Thanksgiving when we flew down to visit. Her attitude toward people who were different had changed. She gushed about her Toyota salesman, Edwin Caldwell. "He, himself delivered the car he sold me. He put a red bow on it. He even took my picture – let me show you." She showed me a picture of herself with a grin the size of Texas, standing in front of her brand-new Toyota.

At that moment, I wondered if maybe I could use Edwin's techniques for convincing others to my point of view. Or pass his tips along to readers. Or use them to make new friends myself?

On the next day's scorching hot Thanksgiving morning at 8 a.m., my husband and I drove to the Quaker Friends School. After parking, we lined up on their track to begin their traditional Thanksgiving five-mile walk/run on dusty forest trails.

Before the race, I was introduced to Edwin. I told him I would be fascinated to learn how he had become such a persuasive car salesperson. And to my surprise, without hesitation, he agreed to tell me his story after I ran the race on this hot, hot, day. In hindsight, it was worth more than the effort!

Edwin Caldwell

This is what he said, "I began my career selling high-end Kirby vacuum cleaner systems door-to-door. I did so well the company, as a reward, moved me to an even ritzier territory."

It was Edwin's nature to scout out new neighborhoods. He continued. "I decided to start selling at a mansion that was bigger than all the rest. I wondered who lived there."

He asked his new sales manager, who responded, "The Grand Wizard of the Klu Klux Klan does, and he doesn't cotton up to Black people. Do not go there for your own sake."

Edwin continued his story. Undeterred, the next day he marched up to the mansion's front door and rang the doorbell chimes, which caused classical music to swirl around the two-story white columns.

The man who opened the door carried himself as if he truly were a Grand Wizard. That is, until he said, "What you doin' knocking at my *front* door! You get off my porch before I..." and the Wizard slammed the door making the house shudder.

Edwin headed back down the front walk with his cleaning equipment. He abruptly stopped. He stood up straighter and pulled back his shoulders. Shook his head. Did an about-face and wended his way past espaliered fig trees to the back door and knocked again.

Mr. Grand Wizard opened the back door and was flabbergasted when he saw it was *him*, again. Edwin quickly said, "Sir, your *brother* was downright impolite, disrespectful, even nasty toward me just now. And I'm a neighbor living right down the road in Chapel Hill!"

"That was me, you damn fool!"

"No sir couldn't 'a been you. You're upstanding, obviously in charge of yourself, and others. You'd never treat another human being like your *brother* just did!"

The whole time Edwin was scraping his feet, preparing to come in. He continued, "I can tell that you like to keep up with current technologies. And this vacuum cleaner system is amazing! Someone curious like YOU should know about it. It'll only take a minute to show you." Edwin paused and leaned forward with a smile, looking to come in.

The Grand Wizard opened the back door a bit wider. Edwin, having rubbed half the soles off his shoes – what with all that scraping – stepped inside.

One conversation led to another. They discussed all the wonderful features of the vac. And sure enough, eventually the Grand Wizard bought a $2,500 vacuum system, a large sum in those days. No doubt the wizard boasted to his friends over Jack Daniels that weekend that his vacuum system was a miracle cleaner.

I imagine, but don't really know, that the wizard might have said to his friends, "You will not believe this bold salesman who came to my front door, I said no, then he went to my back door. Again I said no. But somehow, I ended up with a great new vac system." No doubt they were amazed at that salesman's chutzpah and success.

Since they must have been curious to meet such a determined and persuasive vacuum salesman who didn't understand "no," or because of Mr. Grand Wizard's fantastic cleaning recommendation, Edwin was invited to other KKK member's homes.

And again, I think, without really knowing, that most of them probably soon owned high-end vacuum systems. And they told their friends, and so forth and so on.

The importance of this story to me is not that it is humorous, and illustrates there is good in everyone, or possibly it just makes me feel good. Nor is it important that Edwin has good selling techniques, follow through, and leaves behind satisfied customers.

To me it shouts out, even pleads, that if people of different persuasions and backgrounds would find a way to talk to each other and listen to each other – as the Grand Wizard and Edwin did – and my sister and Edwin did – what a wonderful world this would be!

When I got back home to New Hampshire, I couldn't stop thinking there must be more to Edwin's story. So I called him on the phone and asked, "How did you become such a winning salesman, and turn enemies into friends? Did relatives inspire you? Would you be willing to tell me...please?"

And Edwin, being Edwin, agreed to talk with me. He told

me his family's history, beginning with, "My great-great-great-grandfather Wilson Caldwell was a slave in Chapel Hill, NC. He belonged to David Swain, first President of the University of North Carolina from 1835 to 1868. President Swain had his own children's tutor teach the Wilson family's children, who were slaves. They learned the same lessons that the tutor taught the owner's kids, but separately."

The University of North Carolina president is one of the first known people to reach across racial borders to help Edwin's ancestors.

Edwin Lee Caldwell, a great-great-grandfather, started as a janitor at the DKE fraternity house at UNC in the 1920s. He made $5 a week, but he saved enough money to send his brothers and sisters through college. Helping the situation was that parents of the DKE boys were Hanes Hosiery and Pershing Rifle families.

These parents appreciated that the Black janitor encouraged their sons to learn, accomplish, and to do the right thing in school without their parental guidance. That same great-great-grandfather was made an honorary member of the DKE's and was the only Black face in the yearbook.

He was also the first Black person to buy land in Chapel Hill (13 acres). He built apartments and gave the properties to his brothers and sisters as gifts."

Edwin's great-grandfather, Dr. Edwin Caldwell went to Shaw College, then medical school. He became the doctor who is credited with finding out that pellagra, which causes dementia, diarrhea, and dermatitis, was caused by a lack of niacin, also called vitamin B-3. Medical journals say, "If pellagra is left untreated, it can be fatal."

Edwin's father, Edwin Caldwell Jr. was the first Black person to be a member of the school board in the Chapel Hill, N.C. school district. He had originally chosen Carolina Friends School for his children's earlier education because of the school's Quaker values, commitment to desegregation, and belief that every person holds a piece of the truth.

Our Edwin, the salesman said, "Teachers and founding families of the school, including the Ikenberry family, were supportive of me when I was a student at Quaker Friends." Then, his father on the school board moved Edwin from Friends School to an experimental public school which specialized in pod learning by subject matter.

"Those teachers were amazing," Edwin said. "Except one teacher who didn't want a Black boy in her class. My father made a phone call and the next day she said, 'Edwin, y'all come right on in now, ya hear.'"

Once, Edwin's father was stopped by a policeman. He had a trunk full of cheap liquor he'd just bought. The judge who was called in to handle the case sternly counseled, "You have the right to make one phone call."

"Call the Secretary of the Army," Edwin's father requested.

"Don't kid around with me," the sheriff warned.

But the judge ended up calling the Secretary of the Army,

Kenny Royal, who said, "Let him go! I know Edwin from the DKE's at UNC and he's okay." Then it turned out that same judge and the Army Secretary discovered they had taken classes together at UNC as well.

No one in Edwin's family claims to know who ended up with the liquor, but I have a hunch Edwin would have shared it, or...given it all away.

I was beginning to realize Edwin had impressive role models. But there had to be something more. So I asked, "How do you personally win over your customers? Do you offer them incredibly low prices? Do you slip them a secret potion? Or is it something I haven't thought of?"

Edwin explained his **Life Lesson One**: "When I sell a car to someone, that's not the end of it, but the beginning of our friendship. When the son of a customer was about to start attending Clemson University, I gave the young man a Clemson key ring. And I'll get them tickets to Duke basketball games when Clemson is playing Duke." (If readers don't know, basketball tickets to Duke, my alma mater, are nearly impossible to obtain. Edwin must have convincing connections.)

I asked Edwin to tell me other examples. His **Life Lesson Two:** "Help out whenever you can. When your sister Janet got lost delivering Meals on Wheels to senior citizens, she called me. I came out, helped her find the right addresses, and she delivered the meals, which had perhaps cooled off a bit by then."

Eventually, our daughter Amy was looking for a replacement car and she bought one from Edwin. **Life Lesson Three:** "After a car accident Amy said to Edwin, 'I'm considering buying a used, less expensive car on-line, but alas not from you.' So Edwin looked at the car on the internet and said, 'Amy, buy that used car, that's a great price.' He lost a sale but gained a lifelong friend."

When I saw Edwin at the Thanksgiving road-race the next year, I asked him, "Are you glad you became a car salesman?"

Edwin said, "I do wish sometimes I had become a doctor, like my great grandfather. Nah, it's probably just for ego reasons."

"Why a doctor?" I asked.

"Often strangers will say to me when I first meet them, 'Let me guess, are you a doctor?'"

"I say no."

"'Maybe a preacher then?' is their second guess."

"I say no."

"When I tell them I'm a car salesman, they look disappointed. But after they buy a car from me, usually on someone's recommendation, they seem glad I'm not a doctor or a preacher."

Emilie Spaulding

I have taken away more ideas from Edwin than I anticipated. He has been patient in relating his family stories in person and on the phone.

But the most important lesson I've learned is that if I reach out to strangers and listen to their stories, I learn a new perspective. I have a more open mind to differences. We have become friends. And my new insights are taking me in a direction I had never thought of before.

From our dialogues, we strangers learn to care about each other, respect each other, and share each other's hopes and dreams.

Now, when strangers stump me as to who they are and what they do, one of the things I say to them is, "I'm a writer. But I can't figure out who you are, or what work you do. Just so I can sleep tonight, would you mind giving me some clues, telling me your story, or explaining how you turned out to be who you are?"

To date, no one has refused to talk with me. Best of all, I've learned about people who are different from people I've ever known. And I feel optimistic.

William Jeffries, Peacemaker
JoAnne Jeffries, Autism Law Passer

William Jeffries and JoAnne Jeffries

Bill Jeffries had an NROTC scholarship at the University of Virginia, to be trained for service in the military. But when he expressed his new interest in the peace movement – the University terminated his scholarship and released him. Undeterred, he stayed at the University for the rest of his term. Then, for the rest of his life, he worked for peace, not war, and became a minister.

When Bill became a minister, some members of his church congregations in the Carolinas had objections to their minister's progressive views. His wife, JoAnne says, "Our family moved to different churches quite a bit because of that. When family and friends suggested that Bill not to talk about some of his thoughts, he was hesitant.

Over time he modified his presentation.

Then, an amazing thing happened. At a peace conference, a stranger came up to Bill and asked, "Are you Bill Jeffries?"

"Yes."

The man hesitated. Then finally confessed. "I want you to know, you are the reason I'm at this peace conference. It was my full-time job, when working for the federal government, to tap and listen to all your phone calls for two years. They considered you a peacenik that needed to be watched." The stranger continued, "But...during those same years...a strange thing happened. In the process of listening to you talk about peace and describing what you

William Jeffries and JoAnne Jeffries

were trying to do to help people, I decided to quit my job tapping your phone. I didn't believe in doing that sort of thing anymore. During those years of listening, I was won over to your peaceful point of view. Now, I am also working full time for peace. I couldn't wait to meet you and tell you how much you changed my life! Thank you!"

"Wow! How many other people can make such a claim!" the author of this book says.

When people mentioned Bill Jeffries' name, their voices filled with awe. They'd say, "He was resolute in his support for peace. He supported social justice and citizen involvement. Plus equality for people of all backgrounds. No matter how many people opposed his peaceful views, he never, ever wavered."

Bill was born in July of 1930, in Marietta, Arkansas. His family insists he was born humming and whistling, since they can't remember his not doing so. Sons, Thomas and Jonathan, explain, "I think it was that he sought to make a joyful noise to the Lord. After we kids said our prayers before we got into bed, he would have us chant, 'Now I lay me down to sleep,' followed by another song or two to the heavens."

While getting a Master's in Divinity from Duke University in 1957, he met his future wife JoAnne, who was a junior at Duke. She says, "The instant I met him, I knew...Bill was IT."

When their third son, Kalon was found to be autistic,

JoAnne Jeffries, undeterred, worked with the help of Senators Strom Thurman and Bob Dole to pass a federal regulation that gave help to families with an autistic or developmentally disabled member. For the first time ever, people with these situations would be included in service programs on the state and federal levels.

As Methodist ministers, Bill and his colleagues in the Carolina Conference put forth resolutions to support human and women's rights, peace, and desegregation. Some passed, others didn't.

Bill was out front with causes in which he passionately believed. During the Vietnam War, Rev. Bill worked for the American Friends Service Committee, going on a mission to Vietnam. Back home, he counseled young men who were opposed to taking part in the war. He convinced them not to flee to Canada but to register as a Conscientious Objector at the earliest possible moment. Instead of fighting, they would perform public services for our country. It became a win-win situation.

Sons Thomas and Jonathan remember when growing up – they say it's hard to believe – but they did not notice that people were different – red, yellow, black, white or ethnically mixed. His family acted and treated everyone the same. They remember singing a song, which I, the author, also sang in Georgia at the Lutheran church where I grew up. It went like this, "Red and yellow, black and white, they are precious in his sight. Jesus loves the little children of the world."

Years later, when Bill knew his life was near its end, he began talking and singing a great deal in his native language, German.

JoAnne reports, "He was never morose as he approached the end of his life. Instead, he sang songs while smiling and laughing, including when he died on December 5, 2021."

I asked JoAnne what life lesson she might share as to why she and Bill were so close, and why he could be so happy when he was dying.

JoAnne reports that meditating with Bill was a highlight.

So I asked her, "How does one start meditating?"

"Attend a live Quaker meeting. Go to a meditation conference. Read a meditation book. But do meditation at the same time every day for fifteen minutes. Benefits are it lets love and compassion rise up in you."

But wait, the story doesn't end there. After Bill had passed over, he appeared to her one night and in a clear voice said, "Tell Thomas and Jonathan that I am so proud of them. I love them very much." Joanne seemed to imply it was never too late to make amends for something you might have missed doing in your lifetime, another interesting life lesson.

An amazing 400 people sent cards praising Bill to his family. It seems many hundreds of people had quietly been listening to Bill and his messages. Although Bill was gone, they now cared enough to take the time to tell his family how they felt. And what he had meant to them.

When I asked what other life lessons Bill would have liked to share, members of his family replied without hesitation:

Bill's Life Lesson One would have been a quote from John Wesley who founded the Methodist Church..." Do all the good you can, to everyone you can, for as long as you can."

Joanne believes **Bill's Life Lesson Two** would have been: "Do what you care about whether it is popular or not. People will respect you for sticking to your beliefs, even if they don't share exactly the same opinion."

Bill's **Life Lesson Three** would have been, "Teach your children to follow your example and be strong and unprejudiced toward all others."

In summary I'd like to say, "Rest in peace, Bill. After hearing your story, and in your honor, I hope to follow your life lessons – regardless of whether anyone is listening in on the phone – or not."

Ken

"The secret to success is to do common things, uncommonly well!"

—Ken, Dump and Recycling Manager

Ken, Dump and Recycling Manager

This story begins when the author of this book was a kid of twelve living in small town Georgia. I admired Southern artwork – especially a dead tree with colored bottles turned upside down on its bare branches. When the sun shone through the bottles – blues and greens and brown colors danced on the ground.

I asked Mother if I could make a bottle tree in our yard. She replied with a resounding, "No, Child, a bottle tree screams out that uncouth people live here." Since she won all arguments, I forgot about bottle trees until I was married, and Dick and I lived in Brooklyn Heights.

On weekends, my favorite places to visit were New York City museums. One month, at the Whitney Museum, an artist named Dale Chihuly had an exhibit of his hand-blown glass flowers, artistically placed in the museum's garden.

His hand-blown glass looked to me like a ritzy cousin of our Southern bottle trees. It rekindled my idea.

So, at Lake Winnipesaukee that summer, I finally made my blue bottle tree garden. Moms had passed away recently, living to be 100. I like to believe that even she would have approved of it.

But…where would I find bottles? Rum, liquor, and vodka came in blue bottles. I could become an alcoholic drinking the bottles empty. Or grab bottles secretly from a neighbor's recycling box, out on the street on recycling day. My project was progressing as slowly as a grasshopper trying to jump through dense clover.

Until one Saturday at Lake Winnipesaukee, as I was pitching different bottles into a bin at the summer dump, (there is no trash pickup there), I noticed a guest about to throw a gorgeous blue bottle which would soon smash into bits in the proper metal bin. But rather than grab the customer's arm and perhaps cause him a heart attack, I caught the eye of a young employee, Ken, among the other dump employees I saw there every summer.

"Would you please save me some blue bottles?" I pleaded.

"Shore," he said and saved a huge bin of blue bottles for me the next week.

And the week after.

And the week after that.

"Thanks! I have enough!" I said in appreciation.

Ken's story appears here, not because I need more blue bottles, nor because he is now supervisor of that same dump, but because Ken has excellent life lessons to share. I believe his skills are good enough to run a store on Fifth Avenue in New York City. I was curious how he learned his "people handling skills." Following is what he told me about his life.

Ken was born in 1970 in Groton, Connecticut, at the Naval hospital, and was put up for adoption. His adopting parents were Finnish.

Their neighbor in Connecticut, Mrs. Chandler, a retired

school nurse, gave him a job walking her dog, filling the bird feeder, shoveling the driveway, and doing yardwork. Most importantly, she paid him well and treated him with respect and friendship.

He went to trade school in Danielson, Connecticut to become a carpenter. He loved making and repairing things made of wood. But, because he was much younger than most boys there, the bigger boys bullied him. He made a go cart and the other boys copied him. But Ken won every race because he put cooking oil on the wheel joints. Somehow, he had never got around to mentioning that to the others.

When he went to camp in New Hampshire, he met his wife, and now they are living in New Hampshire.

I asked Ken, "During the pandemic when the line of cars got so long at the dump, and people had to wait half an hour or more just to get through the gate to drop off their trash and recycling, how did you handle that?"

He said, "I wrung my hands...then I simply moved receptacles onto the main road. During this period, residents could dump everything together, therefore only getting out of their car once. We employees would handle the separating after hours. That sped things up tremendously."

I wondered, "How do you and a handful of employees keep 2,300 residents/customers happy?"

"I know all the year-round customer's first names. If they tell me they have a problem, I say, 'Mildred,' for instance, 'why don't we go into my office and let's talk things

Ken

over.' We then sit inside, discuss the problem and possible solutions together, until both of us are happy."

Life Lesson One: "Remember and call everyone by their first name. They will know that you care."

Finally, I asked a tough question, "Tell me about your nastiest customer, but don't tell me his or her name." I thought this would bring forth an interesting, juicy, or maybe even a funny story.

Ken said, "Actually I don't have a nastiest customer. So far, we have resolved each and every problem that has come up."

Now I had the courage to ask a question that was waiting in my head from the beginning. "Do people look down on you because you run a dump, since you oversee their dirty trash, used bottles, and old newspapers and magazines?"

Ken laughed, "When people ask me what I do, I ask them if they want to hear the fancy answer or the plain one."

"'Fancy,' they always say.

"I tell them that I work for a local municipality in middle management.

"'Okay, what's the plain answer?' they ask.

"'I run the local dump,' I tell them."

"Wow, tell me what's the hardest thing you've ever had to solve?"

"I tell everyone the same thing, 'The only hard thing at

the dump is not having enough employees available when it is truly crowded, and the lines are long, and so is the wait.' We all feel bad when that happens."

Life Lesson Two: "The secret to success is to do common things, uncommonly well!"

Stop by our dump if you want to meet a friendly, kind, and capable Dump/Recycling manager. You might also notice, as a result of the dump employees' courtesy, helpfulness, and efficiency, customers themselves seem relaxed, calm, and patient. It is not rare for a resident to signal a different customer to go ahead of them – making even the dump run a fun, interesting, and courteous experience. Ken, Thanks to you and your employees!

An Easter Day Miracle by Memorial Bridge Workers

Memorial Bridge Workers

I was reading the morning paper while glancing out at the roiling water of the Piscataqua River. A headline screamed out to me, "Two Memorial Bridge workers in Portsmouth, NH, gave a 30-year-old local man an incredible Easter gift! It was not a basket of colored eggs, nor a fuzzy white rabbit, nor even a bottle of Pinot Grigio. They saved his life last night on Easter evening."

Incredible! I wondered how it happened. Did he fall or jump? And exactly how did they know when and where to find him? I itched to know the whole story and write about it.

So I asked my husband, Dick, to drive me a couple miles to the Memorial Bridge where the accident happened.

When we got there, the traffic made a roaring noise from dozens of cars thumping across the metal strips on the bottom of the bridge's roadbed.

"Pull over. Stop here!" I called out. There was a small extra lane at the beginning of the bridge. It appeared to be right below the lookout tower. Those bridge workers must enter here to reach their elevated office.

There were metal stairs going up, a metal hand railing, and wire fencing. It was then I noticed the signs: **No Trespassing. Don't Stop. Keep Out**, **Danger.** It also may have said, **This Means You!** But I was here...and I really wanted to find out the whole story...

My husband had reluctantly let me out. So I pushed open

the gate. Then, because of traffic backing up behind him, he had to continue across the bridge to turn around in Maine. "I'll be back!" he shouted. Without time to think, I leapt onto the slightly elevated platform. Ignoring the **KEEP OUT, DANGER, and NO TRESPASSING** signs, I looked up at the office high above, trying to decide what to do. Should I climb up? But I suffer from vertigo and dizziness in high places. Now what should I do?

Fortunately, almost immediately someone shouted down, "Lady, what the heck, (maybe he didn't say heck,) are you doing here?" And some other things I fortunately couldn't hear over the thumping noise of cars rushing by on their way across to Maine."

Since we couldn't hear each other over the traffic, the unidentified man scrambled down the two levels covered by the metal ladder. "Exactly what are you doing here?" Then something a bit nicer, but I couldn't make it out at the noise of traffic roaring by.

He seemed almost as surprised as I now felt that I was standing there. I yelled at him to be heard over the traffic. "I'm a writer. I want to write a story praising the heroic bridge workers who saved that young man's life last night.

"So, I need to talk to one of them to make sure I get the story straight."

He seemed a tiny bit relieved. Then I told him my name and he told me his. "Could you tell me how to get in touch with one of them? I think you guys are terrific." We continued shouting over the traffic roaring by, plus the thumping sounds of cars still bumping on the metal plates of the roadway.

"Don't move," the man shouted to me. "I'll give you his name and phone number. You shouldn't be here you know!" He told me in case I didn't know that. Again, he shook his head in disbelief that I was here on the closed part of the bridge. Quickly, he turned to climb up to the tower again to be on lookout.

"Thanks, I appreciate it!" I yelled, but the din of the traffic drowned me out.

Miraculously, my husband appeared in the car almost immediately, having made the trip to the Maine side of the bridge, where he made a U-Turn to come back, and another U-Turn to where I was. I opened the car door and jumped in.

We had to cross the bridge again and make a U turn to come back in the right direction for home. Dick had gotten to know that bridge pretty well!

Upon reaching home, I took some deep breaths, had a glass of water, and immediately called one of the two rescue fellows. Following is his story of how the two bridge workers kept a stranger from drowning or dying of hypothermia in the freezing-cold river water. Or perhaps floating away forever in the powerful ebb tide of the Piscataqua River between Portsmouth, NH and Kittery, Maine.

Instead of using their real names, these two New

Memorial Bridge Workers

Hampshire Department of Transportation employees insisted that their fellow employees would have cared and saved his life just as well. They'd like the credit for this true Easter Sunday night miracle to go to the whole team. So, at their request, I'll call them, not their real names, but simply...Joe and Tom.

On Easter evening, a young heavy-set fellow had caught Joe and Tom's attention on one of the surveillance cameras, which they watch constantly on their shift.

The young man on the bridge kept stumbling and falling down. He appeared to be intoxicated.

So they continued watching him as they sat in their usual workspace in the elevated bridge tower close to the Portsmouth side of the river. (Workers scan ten cameras which watch different locations on the bridge.)

It is important to remember this would have sadly been a different story, if those same two workers hadn't noticed the man, later falling off the high lift bridge, hitting an abutment, and drifting with the tide toward Maine.

Without a moment's thought, the bridge worker I'll call Joe raced from his high viewpoint down to the bridge surface, across the bridge to the Piscataqua Marina, into Kittery, Maine. His partner, I'm calling Tom, was at the same time calling the local police in Maine and New Hampshire, at each end of the bridge.

Joe kept shouting, hoping the man would respond. He got no answer. Not giving up, he scanned the water, looking back and forth. Finally, he spotted one hand precariously hanging on to the Kittery Marina dock.

Joe hurried down a steep incline, scrambled up a rock stairway, and then scaled a wall to get to get to where the young man was bobbing under, and out of the water. He seemed barely alive.

"Swing your leg up onto the dock," Joe called out to the stranger.

"I can't feel my legs," the man shouted back.

With great effort, Joe pulled the heavy-set lad out of the water while holding on to the seat of his pants, which were dripping icy salt water. With great effort, he got the soggy man onto the dock.

The police had arrived by then on instructions from Tom. They took the water-logged half-frozen young man to the hospital. And miraculously, he survived.

"It was poetic and tragic," Joe said to me. "If we had failed him, I don't know how I would have been able to go back to work the next day and afterward."

He then philosophized about the timing of the event, "Easter Sunday night makes you think of rebirth and the young fella getting a second chance at things. That is what we hope for him. And when he's in a clearer mind, it is our wish that he gets some help.

"Hopefully, the man decides that he was kept alive for a reason. I've never witnessed an event like this. And I hope not to be in this situation again. I can't imagine how it

Memorial Bridge Workers

would feel to lose someone, like a family member."

Eileen Meaney, former public information officer for the NHDOT explained the next day, "DOT members respond to traffic, pedestrian, and motorist incidents. It's an amazing place to work. I know any of our employees would have done the same thing. That's who they are."

Life Lesson One: People who work in safety jobs are proud of what they do, are prepared for the next crisis, and still go home and try to live normal lives with their families and friends.

Special thanks to workers on bridges everywhere. In addition to saving lives, they watch for extremely tall ships that need to have a section of the bridge raised so they can pass under the bridge safely. Now, every time I cross a manned bridge, I say a silent prayer for the workers' safety. And I hope the young heavy set young man who fell off the bridge, has at last found his way.

Peggy, Family Mediator

Peggy, Family Mediator

As the sun rose over Sanibel Island, Florida, the surf roared in and tumbled out, over and over. Brown pelicans flew just above the waves, making a *splat* when they beaked a fish from the salty water. Coming out of the next stucco cabin, I met a woman named Peggy. Thin with blondish hair and a tiny stress line down her forehead, she seemed different from us other tourists. Was it her soothing serenity? Or her kind manner toward two young children she called Pepe and Juanita? Or perhaps it was her transparent love for her sister, Joan, who said, "I'm here to help."

To pass the time, I talked to Peggy about Ding Darling nature preserve, bike paths, and no-seeums – bugs that bite you everywhere and you itch forever. She told me the kids were children to whom she had become a godmother when there were difficulties at their home. To help out, she sponsored them at camp, private school, and one or both spent weekends at her home.

Just then, a dazzling iridescent shell shone from the water. But I left it for someone else since I was intent on finding out Peggy's background, or what she did for a living. I had given up guessing, so I asked, "Why can't I figure out who you are or what kind of work you do? As a writer, it's usually easy for me. But I'm not getting any signals. Would you mind just telling me about yourself and your work?"

Perhaps because we were stalled in time at an almost deserted beach with no appointments, no meetings, or

Peggy

perhaps because she was a kind person, she told me her story. It was more fascinating than any shell, sand dollar, or heron I encountered that week.

Peggy described her work helping divorcing couples find peace, equity, and agreement through mediation.

"How can mediation do that?" I asked, as I slipped a tiny pen and notebook out of my muumuu pocket.

Peggy began, "When couples of any combination decide to split up, they each hire a different, expensive, and nastiest lawyer they can find. Both sides want to get even, exact revenge, or cause financial pain. The two opposing lawyers battle it out, often for years. And most likely the two parties end up hating each other. But when both parties use me as their mediator, in return I love and treat both parties equally."

"How can you possibly *love* opposing sides of anything?" I shook my head disbelievingly.

"Actually, we three try to work as a team. We try to do whatever it takes to reach an equitable solution. We never talk, or email, or phone without all three being present. There are zero private conversations. I think that's the secret to reaching agreement. And it's less expensive than the warring couple hiring two antagonistic lawyers. In my experience, ninety-five percent of cases work out if meditation is used, no matter who the mediator is.

"I like to say, if two parties are about to step into quicksand, a mediator can pull them out before they sink under, and terrible damage is done."

This sounded a lot like the unbelievable Grimm's fairy tales I read when I was little. Fascinated, I asked her, "Could you start at the beginning? Tell me how you ended up choosing this career?"

Peggy said, "When I was eight years old, I wanted to be President of the United States. My wise family counseled, 'Become a lawyer first.' And eventually I did.

"First fact, our family had terrible abuse problems, which involved the whole family. My mother reacted by lowering the shade so the neighbors wouldn't find out. But we dismayed children knew everything."

Peggy continued, "I had to learn how to survive my family situation. I must give credit to my first husband. He helped me heal from my childhood beyond measure. I had years and years of therapy with many different counselors. The only good thing was the skills I learned to survive my past would later serve me and my future clients.

"Now my goal is to help others handle family situations and make their breakup civil, equitable, and as quick as possible."

The thought Peggy left with me was optimistic – that someone who survives a truly trying situation could carry away courage, persistence, and hopefulness. Enough to help them find their way out of any thicket, as she has done.

"Are there any happy endings among your clients?"

"Yes, I was hired by a couple in their late 60s, who after

raising many children of their own and others, decided to divorce. There was no emotional drama nor were there complex finances involved in their mediation.

"Fifteen years later, I ran into the husband coming from his daily visit to the nursing home where his former wife lived with Alzheimer's. Love had endured. Perhaps mediation helped make that possible.

"Another couple with two children graduating from high school and college divided their substantial financial estate equally.

"They had decided, together, not to mention in the mediation, that the wife suffered from alcoholism. They both signed the agreements without rancor or reproach, a hallmark of a good mediation solution. In saying goodbye, the husband wished his wife success in her recovery."

How classy, I thought.

"In mediation of a divorce between military couples — often one is a military nurse or doctor, and the other is a pilot or commander or soldier. Their shared wartime experience is frequently displayed in their gentleness and generosity toward one another. Before, I had thought military breakups would be the most difficult.

"I've mediated married couples who have found the courage to come out as gay or lesbian. I am speechless to express the beauty of witnessing the shared experience of one or both having the courage to risk everything in taking that step."

We paused the conversation long enough to spray on #30 suntan lotion and bug spray for the nasty no-seeums. If only she had a good solution for the cause of everyone itching all night.

She continued, "If both sides are willing to talk to each other, the settlement can sometimes happen in four to six two-hour meetings. In other cases, perhaps where one or both won't talk, the sessions can drag on for months, years, or they may never agree."

"Peggy," I asked, "Is there an awful side, tell me."

"Yes, there are clients who scream, swear, even throw things at each other. Others lie and try to intimidate or hide their affairs or hide how much money they have or hide addictions. In those cases, we need to repeatedly create a space for them to feel safe enough to trust the process. They need to feel they will be heard and respected. It takes consistent kindness, good math, and legal skills. These measures could help them enjoy the benefits of an equitable agreement.

"Their other option is to maintain the status quo and remain miserably married or they can hire two hostile attorneys. With the thought of a long-term hostile conflict, many people decide to try to mediate...successfully."

Peggy continued, "A variation on couple mediation is when a company is trying to work out the line of succession from the founder to new management. Family members in several generations could be involved. Mediation solves problems and lubricates the wheels of change *if* all will speak to each other."

"How much does this cost, roughly?"

"My prices for any mediation are on a sliding scale, and veterans get a discount."

I save the hardest questions for the end of an interview. Perhaps so my victim – I mean interviewee – won't jump up and say, "That's it! No more questions! We're finished!" Then we won't get the whole story. And although I thought this question might be one Peggy would be reluctant to answer. I asked her anyway.

"Peggy…do you have any free and clear ideas about how married couples can work out their differences? Most couples must have some aggravating circumstances."

She laughed.

I continued, "And not have to get to the point of using a mediator like you? Or not having to get so far apart as to hire two separate divorce lawyers?"

To my joy, Peggy nodded and shared this sage, **Life Lesson One:** "If one of a married party says, early on, 'Let's go to counseling and both agree, that's the best hope."

Life Lesson Two: "If one of the partners doesn't like the counselor, just keep choosing another until you find the right one. Just keep talking and talking."

Life Lesson Three: "Each partner must take a risk and tell the other person the truth when something bothers her or him, even if it hurts. The receiving partner should remain calm and listen and not interrupt. Then they reverse roles, and the second partner takes his/her risk and tells her or his side, and the first partner listens. This can be a bonding opportunity."

A week later I called Peggy to get some of her wider thoughts. "Peggy, since you are so wise about all kinds of people, what is your advice for the world in general, and/or my readers?" She didn't hesitate to tell me **Life Lesson Four**: "Forgive quickly, laugh at yourself, and let people make their own mistakes without comment or judgment from you."

Life Lesson Five: "Be kind, smile at three people or more a day, or as often as you can." Peggy may not have become President, but she has become a catalyst in thousands of situations where people have worked out conflicts, found solutions, and moved forward. Worthy goals all. And the best part is that all of Peggy's advice is free to me and you – at least the bill hasn't arrived in the mail...yet.

* You can receive further information on mediation services in your state if you google www.meditationservices.com, or ask Alexa. I wish you the best of luck in all of your relationships.

Jean Royer

"No matter how hard your start,
Keep doing what you love, and
things will turn out okay!

—Jean Royer, Blueberry Angel

Jean Royer

One misty, moist, morning as we drove past rustic cabins on a twisty two-lane road in New Hampshire, my husband and I saw a quaint hand-painted sign saying *Angelic Farm*. Small angel statues stood at attention in the niches of the stone gate and on tree stumps in nearby woods. Serenity hung in the air. Ah-h-h.

A second sign by a stack of firewood on the road's edge called out, *"Take an armful-three dollars-or two armfuls for five."* This would be tempting to passersby who would soon be building a campfire. Whoever operates this place must be a trusting soul since they left the definition of *armful* up to us; I thought.

A third sign read, *PYOB, (pick your own berries)*. We were curious, so we turned onto Angelic Farm Road and wandered through a glade of rustling pines. Clouds floated overhead in shades of blue and white. Woods opened onto a broad field of rows of blueberry bushes.

A fourth sign on the shed said, "Pick a quart – eight dollars." Even the honor-system money box fit the calming ambiance.

A smiling man with graying hair, dressed in a straw sun hat, tee shirt, khaki shorts, work boots, and high socks, stood up from his bench near a supply shed. "Welcome, I'm Jean."

He gave us buckets with strap handles and showed us ripe rows to pick where no one else would be around. Was this real? Were we dreaming? We sprayed our hands with disinfectant hanging from a rope on a nail.

Six-foot-tall bushes drooped under the weight of clusters of berries. Dark blue berries were our target. Those in shades of green could wait.

We put a bucket strap over one arm, held the bucket under the bunches, and pulled clumps of berries gently down with the other. *Plunk,* blue orbs bounced off the bucket bottom.

Jean talked about something different each time we returned to pick berries. He didn't match my stereotypical image of the farmers in my family, who were rightly consumed with crop yield, getting rid of insects, weather forecasts, and food prices. Often, I asked Jean to tell me what he did before he ended up with 20 acres on Lake Winnipesaukee, a house and barn, and fields of blueberries. After a while, he told me this challenging story.

"Seventy-five years ago, my French-Canadian forebears lived in Massachusetts. My grandfather was a custodian and my grandmother a stay-at-home mom. My mother left school at 15 to become a shoe sewer in a Lowell mill. My father started as a cook at Beaudry's Diner in Manchester, N.H.

"Four months before I was born, World War II began in the United States when Japan attacked Pearl Harbor. It was a period of terrible anxiety. That was why when I was born on March 4, 1942, I was crying. Mother said I continued to cry a lot in those days. I've always been quick to do so. Frankly, people who are continually effervescent, light-hearted, and effervescent make me suspicious," Jean confessed.

Jean went on: "My father got a job as a welder at the Boston Navy Yard two hours away, and my mother also worked.

"I was shuffled around to neighbors' apartments before and after school. I never knew where I'd end up. This lasted until I was old enough to become a latch-key kid, letting myself in and out of our house, where I'd stay alone till my parents came home.

"The summer when I was six and my parents were still working. I went to sleepaway camp during the week. When I found some loose boards around the camp property, Miss Alice, the owner and camp director, let me build a racing cart.

"Back home, the neighborhood boys decided to build carts like mine. I always won the races. I never told anyone why – until now. It was because I put Crisco shortening on the axles and wheels before every race, shh." (Looking back to Ken's story it seems that this was a popular ploy for enterprising young boys.)

He went on. "Being an only child, I had no siblings to teach me the ins and outs of getting along, sharing, and how to give and take. I learned everything on my own, you might say by trial and error – and there were a few errors.

Jean Royer

"At my first job at 13, when I was at the top of a tall ladder washing stained glass windows of a church, I asked Frere' Joyal, my boss, to hand me supplies a couple times. Soon he said, 'I'm not your servant, get them yourself!' In that moment of unpleasantness, I learned to be independent, and I follow that style to this day.

"At 15, I was building boxes at church to send supplies to Haitian missionaries. There were lots of hit fingers, but the brighter side is that from that experience I learned I loved to build, to create, and to figure out solutions.

"In June 1959, I graduated from high school and went one semester to Lowell Technological Institute. I decided perhaps I wasn't ready for college and mother too quickly agreed and supported the idea that I make money by finding work. Gerry Roberts, who had competed against me to be the fastest typist in high school, convinced me to train to become a keypunch operator with the IRS in Massachusetts.

"So Gerry, my former rival, had a change of heart, and drove us both to work since I didn't have a car. Being fast typists, Gerry and I stood out.

"Now I could buy a '57 Oldsmobile convertible –a babe-magnet I thought – and it was. Father Bourgeois asked me to pick up a young woman, Jeannine Belley, to bring her several times to the Young Christian Workers meetings. I don't know whether Father B. planned for us to get together, or whether he was just very wise.

Emilie Spaulding

"The war in Vietnam was heating up, and Uncle Sam asked me to have a physical exam. I passed. Then the Air Force Reserve saved me from going to war in exchange for a six-year one-weekend-a-month commitment after basic training. Jeannine organized a surprise going away party. I must have been crazy to tell her to date others while I was away.

"In the Air Force, I learned how to use every piece of equipment in data processing, such as collators, duplicators, sorters, calculators, and tabulators. They all used punch cards then. I graduated first in my class.

"But I still didn't realize my life would be changed forever because of my problem-solving data-processing skills. With the free G.I. bill when I got out, I studied philosophy and still can't read enough about it. My recommendation is to read *The Truth Shall Set You Free* by Emery Tang, to spark your philosophical interest as well.

"One day while passing Tew Mac airport in Tewksbury, Massachusetts, I mentioned to Jeannine I always wanted to fly a plane. Her response, as always, was 'That's a good idea.'"

Life Lesson One: "Marry a wife who will encourage you to do what you love, regardless of how foolish it seems in that moment. After getting a pilot's license, I would fly our family to different locations on vacation. I got my commercial pilot's license so I could fly bigger planes. It is hard for me to describe the feeling one gets flying a plane in the unending sky with clouds scudding by."

"Did Jeannine know back then how far I'd stay with flying? Probably. She never said she was afraid to fly with me, even on long-distance trips. I've never asked what her true thoughts were in my learning days.

"I never had a dull moment to sit around and relax. Technology kept changing as it's wont to do. The company I worked for went out of business and I was out of a job just as we were about to have our fifth child!

"As always, with Jeannine's encouragement I started my own company – Data Professionals. I loved to figure out computing problems for companies like Hertz and Avis, on down to local town clerks, funeral directors, and churches. That forty years of data processing flew by.

"I retired in 1999 at age fifty-seven, and we bought south-facing real estate which we thought would be a key survival factor in this frozen north. Our lives changed when Roy, a close friend, came by, reached down with his bare hand, and fingered our new property's dirt, which was believed to have been a sheep farm.

"'Heck, you could grow anything you wanted in this,' he said. Local friend, 'Apple Ed' Powell suggested blueberries. We bought a few bushes, which have expanded to 730. Because some blueberries fall to the ground, we bought chickens for manure, which made the blueberries thrive – an unplanned cycle of good fortune.

"A most important fact is we have three different seasonal berries. Dukes ripen early; Blue Crop is ready mid-summer. Elliot's ripen later in the season. Picking starts shortly after the Fourth of July and ends in September. There's never a slow season."

Jean concluded, "Visitors give us high ratings on tourist sites, so our blueberry business is busy. In the distant future, we might be looking for a young family to buy and carry Angelic Farm into the future."

Jean told me "This is the most satisfying work. Because of the lake setting, the quiet where I can meditate and think new thoughts and have the joy of meeting wonderful people. It helps me keep going seven days a week."

"Not a day off – yikes!"

Jean Royer's **Life Lesson Two**: "No matter how hard your start in life may be, keep doing what you love, and things will turn out okay."

Life Lesson Three: "Choose a life partner that you would like to live with for sixty years or more."

We customers hope that Jean will continue the blueberry farm's angelic traditions for a long time. And when you see a PYOB sign on any roadside, turn in and you will enjoy fruit that you picked in your freezer all winter.

EPILOGUE

It is my hope that you will incorporate many of these life lessons into your own lives and will find them helpful.

I have learned a great deal from the thoughtful strangers who gladly shared their time, lessons, and deepest thoughts with us. It was a pleasure meeting, and talking with all of you.

And thanks to the readers who will try some of these heartfelt suggestions, and tell others about the book and its messages.

Appreciated!

Emilie Spaulding, *Author*

www.ingramcontent.com/pod-product-compliance
Lightning Source LLC
Chambersburg PA
CBHW020948090426
42736CB00010B/1312